THE GUIDE TO DUE DILIGENCE

"any deal, any size, any location"

Nathan Tabor

Copyright © 2018

All rights reserved. No part(s) of this book/guide may be reproduced, stored in a retrieval system, or transmitted in any form or by any means, electronic, mechanical, photocopying, recording, scanning, or otherwise without the prior written permission of the publisher.

Table of Contents

The Guide to Due Diligence 1
   5 Rules of Due Diligence 1
      Rule #1: 1
      Rule #2: 1
      Rule #3: 2
      Rule #4: 2
      Rule #5: 2

Due Diligence: "Verify Everything" 4
   American with Disabilities Act (ADA) 4
   Administrative Offices 4
   Animals 4
   Appliances 5
      CRITICAL TIP: Stealing Appliances 5
   Appraisals 6
   Asbestos 6
   Bank Statements 7
   Bathrooms 7
   Bed Bugs 7
   Certificates of Occupancy 8
   Current Owner's Loan 8
   Drainage 9
   Dumpster Pads and Fences 9

CRITICAL TIP: Cost of Hauling 10
Electrical Plugs 10
  CRITICAL TIP: Safety 10
Electrical Wiring 11
Electrical Breaker Boxes 11
Electrical Meter Packs 11
Elevators 12
  CRITICAL TIP: Meter Packs 12
Environmental: Phase I, II, and III per Wikipedia.com
.... 13
  CRITICAL TIP: Environmental Issues 14
Exterior Lighting 15
Evictions last 12 Months 16
  CRITICAL TIP: Verify, Verify, Verify 16
Fire Code 17
Fire Extinguishers 17
Fire Hydrants 17
Flood Zone 18
Flooring 18
Gas vs Electrical 18
GFI 19
Health Code 19
Hot Water Heaters 19
HVAC Systems 19

Housing Complaints 20
Insurance 21
   CRITICAL TIP: Out of Pocket 22
Kitchen 23
   CRITICAL TIP: #1 Reason 23
Laundry Facility 23
Leases 24
Lis Pendens 24
Mailboxes 25
Maintenance Materials 25
Market-Related Research 26
Mold Issues 26
Playgrounds / Swimming Pools 27
Police Reports 27
   CRITICAL TIP: Police Officer 28
Property Taxes 28
Rent Roll 29
   CRITICAL TIP: Rent Roll Nightmare 29
Range Hoods 30
Roaches 30
Roads: Local and State 30
Roof Structures 31
   CRITICAL TIP: Documentation 31
Security Deposits 31

Sewage 31

Sidewalks 33

Signage 34

Tenant Applications 34

    CRITICAL TIP: Tenant Screening 34

Termites 35

    Toilets 35

Vacant Units 36

Vendor Contracts 36

Water Damage 36

Work Orders 37

Zoning Letter 37

    CRITICAL TIP: My Nightmare! 37

PERSONAL STORY: What You Can't See… 39

Documents to Request from the Seller (if applicable) 42

About Nathan Tabor 44

Services Offered 46

Disclaimer 49

The Guide to Due Diligence

Due diligence *will* make you or break you! Due diligence is **CRITICAL** to your success as a real estate flipper or investor. Done well, and you can operate a successful business. Not done well, and it could be the NAIL in your coffin. The time when you are purchasing and flipping a property is your time to identify all the issues and problems at hand. Then determine the necessary steps to fix them before you can no longer recoup your earnest money.

When doing your due diligence, it is critical to do it right. Here are 5 rules that will help you avoid mistakes and make your deal stronger.

5 Rules of Due Diligence

Rule #1: Make sure all communication is in writing. Whether the communication is through your broker, the seller's broker, the seller, the attorney or the garbage man — put it in writing.

Rule #2: Itemize all needed documents in an addendum to the purchase contract or LOI. Stipulate when each document is due and specify the dates for walking all units and the entire property.

Rule #3: As you start this process, build out a "jacket" on the deal. A jacket is a notebook or folder that you use to store every document. With a good organization system, you won't waste time searching for lost materials or ask the seller to provide them again.

Rule #4: Build out your own P&L and expenses to operate the property. Review what has been provided to you, but assume every number is wrong until you verify it with proper documentation. If you can't verify a number, then you will need to research and find a way to verify it. If you still can't verify a number, then increase that number by 50% to cover yourself for any unexpected contingencies.

Rule #5: Determine the real cost to renovate and stabilize the property. If you don't feel comfortable with this process, consult with someone who can help you.

Remember, real estate contracts have four corners. Meaning once you close the deal, the contract is binding and what's contained in those four corners is it. There are NO returns or exchanges!

Now there can be one asterisk in this situation. If you can prove intentional fraud on the part of the seller, then you can sue on this ground. However, I've been there and it's not easy to prove. Plus, it's very costly to hire an attorney to pursue the matter. The best thing for you is to become a due diligence expert or hire a due diligence expert.

Due Diligence: "Verify Everything"

During your due diligence period, you need to check EVERY aspect. Below are the things I check and verify when purchasing a property. Remember, "Verify, Verify, Verify and then Verify again!" Let's get started!

American with Disabilities Act (ADA)

Does the property need to be ADA complaint, and if so what areas? If you believe there are any ADA issues, make sure these are addressed before the end of due diligence.

Administrative Offices

Is there an office on site? Is it located within in a model unit? If so, you have to subtract the potential rent from the gross income.

Animals

Animals are a gift from God. Personally, I've always had a dog or dogs in my life. But animals in a rental property create a unique situation. Is the owner a responsible or irresponsible pet owner? After a few years in the business, I had to make a hard decision. The decision was to not allow animals in the units. The damage caused by precious pets can be quite expensive. You will also want to check with your insurance company about any restrictions on animals.

Appliances

When doing your due diligence, you need to know when various items in the units where last replaced. A used set of appliances will cost around $400 and will probably last a few years. A brand new set of appliances will cost around $900 at one of the big box stores. Your rent and tenant base should determine the type of appliances you purchase. If you are selling the property, then use comparable appliances to the comps.

CRITICAL TIP: Stealing Appliances

One of the frustrating aspects of owning rental properties is when tenants steal appliances. Most magistrate offices will NOT issue an arrest warrant if you don't have the unit serial number. And the amount of the claim doesn't make sense to turn it into insurance. So make sure you write down the serial numbers of the appliances in each unit. Another option is to rent units without appliances, and the tenant can supply and take care of their own appliances.

Appraisals

Is a current appraisal available? Has the owner or bank completed an appraisal in the last 6–12 months? The older an appraisal gets, the more useless it becomes. If an appraisal has been completed recently, ask your bank if you can pay a fee to update the current appraisal instead of having a new one completed. It will save you time and money. Now, make sure you read the current appraisal, study the comps, look for any red flags, and make sure your numbers make sense with the value. If the property is worth $1,000,000 and it needs $100,000 of renovations and you are paying $850,000, then you aren't going to make any money.

Asbestos

Traditionally, you will find asbestos in tile flooring and potentially in popcorn ceilings. Having an expert examine the property is highly recommended, if not mandatory. Learn more at https://www.epa.gov/asbestos/us-federal-bans-asbestos

Bank Statements

How do you verify income? Simple! Ask for Bank Statements! This is the ONLY way to verify how much money is being brought in by the property. If the rent roll says $30,000 a month and the bank statements show $15,000 in deposits, then something is not right.

Bathrooms

What is the condition of the bathtub? Can you restore it, install a wall surround or does it need to be torn out? Check the cabinet, sink, faucet and for water damage under the sink. Look for newly replaced cabinet bottoms.

Bed Bugs

Bed bugs are expensive to treat! Look through city complaints and work orders to identify any potential bed bug issues. Talk with tenants and management as well. Does the property have a history of bed bugs? Check with local companies and get quotes on the cost to treat bed bugs if needed. Traditionally companies will give you a better rate on bed bug treatment when they do your insect treatment.

A 2-bedroom, 1-bath unit will cost between $350 and $600 to treat, and most cities require the landlord to pay for the treatment. Even if a tenant is required to pay, what are you going to do if they refuse? Bed bugs spread quickly from one unit to the next. It is much easier and cost effective to treat on unit rather than 50% of your property. The best thing you can do when bed bugs arrive is to address the issue immediately.

Certificates of Occupancy

You will need Certificates of Occupancy for all units in order to have a meter set by the power company. If power has been off for more than a year, then you will need an electrician.

Current Owner's Loan

What is the status of the owner's current loan? Will the bank let you assume the loan? Or would the bank be interested in financing the deal for you?

The answer is always 'no' until you ask! So don't be afraid to structure a deal that works for you and the seller. It might not be a traditional structure, but if you can get the deal done and the numbers make sense then approach the bank with your offer.

Keep the following items in mind when structuring a loan:

- Terms
- Assumable
- Appraisal
- Insurance
- Bank interest in financing another loan

Drainage

Walk the property and look for areas where rain water is running off the property. You will notice rutting, loss of grass, and issues with ditches. Storm water runoff is a leading cause of water pollution. It is caused when water runs off solid surfaces and collects various pollutants, such as pesticides, oil, and other sediments. Runoff can affect both water and aquatic life. The fix is simple, but costly. So, negotiate with the seller to fix the issue.

Dumpster Pads and Fences

Most older properties don't have dumpster pads or fences. However, most waste management companies require that you have a concrete dumpster pad and pull-up area so their trucks don't damage your parking lot. Most cities now require dumpsters to be contained within a three-sided fence.

CRITICAL TIP: Cost of Hauling

What's the cost of hauling off all the waste after demolition?

Electrical Plugs

Purchase an outlet tester for $5 and use it on every outlet. The cost to rewire a unit can be in the thousands of dollars. After purchasing properties, I've found units where half the plugs didn't work. But during due diligence, the tenant or previous owner didn't disclose this. The burden and cost were left to me.

CRITICAL TIP: Safety

One of the scariest moments I've ever had flipping rentals was the afternoon I walked into a unit on the second floor and found two men in a bedroom. Upon a quick glance around, it looked like a maze had been dug into the sheetrock. These men had removed almost every bit of electrical wiring in the unit and were in the process of stripping it down for the copper. So, I found myself standing between them and the exit. I politely said hello and told them to have a nice day.

Then I left and called the police. Unfortunately, they were already gone when the police arrived. The lesson learned here is to always be careful when walking a property by yourself!

Electrical Wiring

Copper Wiring or Aluminum Wiring: Does the property have copper or aluminum wiring? Copper is the preferred type of wiring. It is safer for use and traditionally is cheaper to insure. I've had insurance companies require "pig tails," be put on aluminum wiring before they would write an insurance policy.

Electrical Breaker Boxes

Do the breaker boxes have breakers or glass twist fuses? If glass twist fuses are currently being used, upgrade to more modern breakers during the renovation or plan on deducting the cost to upgrade from your selling price.

Electrical Meter Packs

Have a licensed electrician inspect meter packs and confirm with the power company that meters can be set for any vacant units. Meter packs can cost anywhere from $800–$2,200 each, plus the cost of running lines to the pole and rewiring the unit if necessary.

If a unit hasn't had power for more than a year, or a specific period, you will be required to have a licensed electrician pull a permit and inspect the unit. Check with your local building inspector for exact time.

Elevators

Does the property have any elevators? Have the elevators been inspected per state code? Missing this WILL be very expensive!

CRITICAL TIP: Meter Packs

Check if the meter packs are stamped with a utility company name. Most meter packs installed during the 60s and 70s are property of the utility company, and the utility company is responsible for their upkeep. On two properties I purchased, the utility company had to replace $80,000 and $50,000 of meter packs. In return, I signed a document, which stated that moving forward the meter packs belonged to the property.

Environmental: Phase I, II, and III per Wikipedia.com

Phase I Environmental Site Assessment is a report prepared for a real estate holding that identifies potential or existing environmental contamination liabilities. The analysis, often called an **ESA**, typically addresses both the underlying land as well as physical improvements to the property.

Phase II Environmental Site Assessment is an "intrusive" investigation which collects original samples of soil, groundwater or building materials to analyze for quantitative values of various contaminants. This investigation is normally undertaken when a Phase I ESA determines a likelihood of site contamination. The most frequent substances tested are petroleum hydrocarbons, heavy metals, pesticides, solvents, asbestos, and mold.

Phase III Environmental Site Assessment is an investigation involving remediation of a site. Phase III investigations aim to delineate the physical extent of contamination based on recommendations made in Phase II assessments. Phase III investigations may involve intensive testing, sampling, and monitoring, "fate and transport" studies, and other modeling, as well as the design of feasibility studies for remediation and remedial plans. This study normally involves the assessment of alternative cleanup methods, costs, and logistics. The associated reportage details the steps taken to perform site cleanup and the follow-up monitoring for residual contaminants.

When looking at environmental assessments, find out if there are any current or past issues. Have any business been located by the property that could have caused issues, such as dry cleaners or gas stations? Ask the current owner if he/she has had any environmental studies completed in the past.

CRITICAL TIP: Environmental Issues

Any time you purchase a property, you are purchasing any and all liabilities that come with the property—whether you know about them or not.

Banks traditionally require a Phase I before loaning money on a property. If the Phase I results in any red flags, then a Phase II will be required. A typical Phase I will cost between $1,500-5,000, but I've paid as much as $8,000 because of the property size and quick turn-around needed.

When you are paying cash for a property or owner financing a property, this can be very dangerous grounds. A Phase I isn't required in this type of transaction; but if you don't get a Phase I, you are assuming all environmental issues.

This happened to me on a property for which I paid all cash. After closing, I was notified by the NC Department of Environmental and Natural Resources (NC-DENR) that there was a potentially serious Issue on the property.

More than 15 years had passed since a dry-cleaning store had been torn down that was located across the road. The dry-cleaning solvent was flagged as having potentially contaminating the soil. Once the bank discovered this issue, they put the package on hold until the issue was resolved. It took more than 12 months for NC-DENR to drill holes, run tests, and clear the property. Thankfully I was in the property right and this didn't cause much trouble other than time. Had I been on a bigger deal and had an issue with NC-DENR testing, it could have caused a lot of financial problems and stress.

Exterior Lighting

Is the exterior lighting in place? Does it work? Who pays? If the lights are working, they are either being paid by the property or by the city (if they are on city property). If they aren't working, there is a 50/50 chance the lights are maintained by the local city but nobody has reported them as being out. If the lights aren't on city property, then call the local power company to see if they maintain them. If neither the city nor the power company maintains the lights, then find out the cost of maintaining them and the cost of power.

Evictions last 12 Months

Evictions tell the story. The last 12 months of evictions will tell you how often the units are turning over. With that information in hand, compare it to the rent roll and create a spread sheet marking when a unit went vacant and when someone else moved in. If you want to cover yourself well, go back two to five years for a crystal-clear picture of how stable or unstable the property has been.

CRITICAL TIP: Verify, Verify, Verify

The function of due diligence is to verify, verify, verify… and then to verify again. You can't verify things too many times. Remember, this isn't a game or a hobby. It's real money, with real guarantees, with real consequences.

Fire Code

Contact the local Fire Marshall to see if there are any issues or complaints on the property.

Fire Extinguishers

Are fire extinguishers required? Are fire sprinkles required? If so, are there any issues with current system?

Fire Hydrants

Where are the fire hydrants located? Who pays for upkeep? Before purchasing a 56-unit property on 13 acres, I assumed that all fire hydrants were maintained by the fire department and local government. Well, that isn't true. After closing, I was told that all fire hydrants were on private property and thus my responsibility.

Since the road in the development wasn't maintained by the city, neither were the fire hydrants. The road was paved and even had a name, but since the fire hydrants were installed on private property, the waterline and the fire hydrants were the financial responsibility of the property. Without working fire hydrants, the insurance company wouldn't have insured the property.

Fire Hydrants can cost $1,000 to $6,500 to replace, plus any water lines and permits that have to be pulled.

Flood Zone

Is the property in a Flood zone? You can visit www.floodsmart.gov to learn more by entering the property address. This government website will tell you the cost of flood insurance as well. If just a small corner of the property is in a flood zone, most banks will require flood insurance on the property. If you don't research this in advance, then you wouldn't know this until after your due diligence time is up and your earnest money is no longer retractable.

Flooring

What shape is the flooring in? Over the years I've used vinyl squares and laminate wood flooring. Both are good products but not the best for rentals. Vinyl plank flooring is a bit more expensive but worth the extra money.

Gas vs Electrical

Does the heat pump and stove use gas or electric? What is the cost of maintaining the gas pipes? Does this increase or decrease the tenants utility bills?

GFI

Check the bathroom and kitchen. Do they have GFI plugs? If not check with your electrical contractor. Your insurance company could require GFI plugs.

Health Code

Health code violations normally don't apply to rental properties unless a tenant is running a catering business illegally out of their unit.

Hot Water Heaters

You will need a licensed plumber and electrician to replace a hot water heater. The cost to replace a 40-gallon hot water heater can average about $1,200 each.

HVAC Systems

HVAC means Heating, Ventilating, and Air Conditioning. HVAC is your central heating and air. Make sure that you have a licensed HVAC contractor inspect all units. You will also want to discuss the type of Freon currently being used and if any upgrades or replacements are required. If so, what type of Freon will be required?

Housing Complaints

Call or visit your local housing authority and request the last 12-24 months of housing complaints. If you don't know how to do this, you can either ask the seller to provide them, have your broker request it or hire a consultant to help you. Without these complaints, you will NOT have a full picture of what's been going on at the property.

Here is an example of what you can find. If over a 12-month period the bottom units have complained numerous times about their toilet or bathtub or both backing up with sewage, then you can assume one of two things. Either a tenant is flushing things down the toilet and stopping it up OR there is an issue with the sewage pipes. The first one is costly but can be fixed by changing out the tenant once you identify the source. The other could cost you a few thousand dollars to tens of thousands of dollars. If your property is sitting on a foundation and the pipe has collapsed under a unit, which means you will have to remove a portion of the foundation and replace the pipe. If it is collapsed in several places, you could have to replace the entire pipe. And during the time period the work is being done, you will have to move the tenants out—which means lost rents.

In the meantime, you will also identify the problem tenants. If a tenant has his or her front door kicked in by a "visitor," you as the landlord are required to fix it. You can bill them for the damage, but you have to fix the door first or the city will cite you and/or levy a fine. Look through the complaints and see who has had physical damage to their unit. Broken doors usually signifies a unit whose tenants have frequent fights. Replacing flooring and door jams due to damage most likely means a dog is often left in the unit unattended.

To recap, these complaints will give you a clear picture of two things:

- Condition of the units or lack there of
- Type of tenant base

Insurance

Just like getting points on your driver's license, a property is tagged with insurance claims. The more claims a property has, the higher the insurance will be. During your due diligence time, you need to get quotes from insurance companies. If the current owner has had several claims within the last 12 months, it could make the policy cost increase. When you are getting a quote, the insurance company will request three to five years of loss runs: reports provided by insurance companies that document the claim activity on past policies. Past claims can drastically increase premiums.

Ask the current owner who is insuring the property. How much is the annual premium? What is the deductible? Make sure you request a quote based on the deductible your bank will require. A deductible is the amount the owner is responsible for when making a claim. Let's say your deductible is $25,000 and you file a claim for a total repair cost of $50,000. This means that the first $25,000 is covered by the owner and the insurance company will cover the remaining $25,000.

When buying insurance, the lower the deductible the higher the cost. Shop the policy and find the best rate because damage **will** happen.

CRITICAL TIP: Out of Pocket

There will be damage to the property that will have to be covered out of pocket.

For example, a tenant may cause a fire while cooking in the kitchen resulting in about $5,000 in damage. Even with a low deductible of $10,000, it wouldn't be wise to turn this claim into your insurance company. You would make the loss runs with a claim, but the insurance company wouldn't cover any of the expense.

Kitchen

Examine the condition of the cabinets, countertop, sink and faucet. This area is one of the most expensive areas to renovate. Open up the cabinet under the sink and visual inspect for water damage. If there is water damage you need to determine if it has reached the floor or wall.

CRITICAL TIP: #1 Reason

One of the top reasons that a tenant doesn't rent a unit is because the kitchen and bathroom(s) aren't clean and or renovated.

Laundry Facility

Where is the closest laundry mat? Most properties don't have washer and dryer hookups. Most prospective tenants will want to know where the closest laundry facilities are.

Leases

Leases are critical for many different reasons. But the most important reason from a flipping standpoint is where in the lease is the tenant? Most leases are 12-month leases, and during this time frame you can't go up on rents. When purchasing a property, tell the owner upfront that you prefer they NOT go out and get every tenant to sign a new lease. If your goal is to raise the rents, this will be unattainable until the current lease expires.

Need a lease? Visit Docs.NathanTabor.com to learn more.

Lis Pendens

lis pen·dens (lis ˈpendenz) Noun: a pending legal action, or a formal notice of this Lis Pendens are used by those who having pending litigation against the property, by housing authorities to show open complaints or city fines owed or by utility bills owed. Title companies will generally not provide title insurance on properties that have Lis Pendens recorded against them. But discovering this information lets you peer into the past or current issues at the property.

You can obtain this information through several means:

- A report from the seller
- Register of Deeds office
- An Attorney pulls the records
- Paying for the title policy before due diligence is over (not recommended)

Mailboxes

Are there any current mailboxes on site? Who pays for upkeep? What's the cost to repair? Every property has some type of mailbox, perhaps similar to this aluminum mail box. I've never owned a property where I wasn't responsible for providing them. These multi-unit mailboxes can be VERY expensive! The local Post Master with the United States Postal Service (USPS) will maintain both the locks and keys on the mailboxes. When a tenant vacates a unit, the USPS will charge $15 dollars to change out the lock and $5 per additional key. So we made this cost part of the lease, and the tenant is required to set up their mailbox lock and key with the local post office.

Maintenance Materials

Are maintenance materials stored on site? If so, are they part of the purchase agreement?

Market-Related Research

When purchasing a property, you have to consider the surrounding market. Specialized companies can provide you with this specific market research.

You can also opt to perform market research on your own. If so, be sure to cover the following areas:

- Property location
- Surrounding property conditions
- Stop in local businesses to ask what they've heard about the property.
- Check out other rental properties in the area.
- What have other properties sold for in the last 6-12 months?
- Are businesses opening or closing in the area?
- Speak with the local housing inspector because they will have one of the best perspectives on the property.

Mold Issues

Whether you see mold or not, I recommend testing for it. The fastest and most economical way to test for mold is a $10 mold test with a $40 lab fee. You can purchase the test online or at any hardware store. Simply place the test in a unit for 24-48 hours, and then mail the test to the designated laboratory. If it comes back positive, your next step is to call a mold expert and get a quote on the cost to remediate.

Playgrounds / Swimming Pools

Playgrounds and swimming pools are a much-requested amenity by tenants. In flipping Class C properties, I found that having these items only cause your insurance to go up due to potential liability. But this cost and liability didn't allow me to raise the rents. If something costs you money and doesn't allow you to raise rents then why have it? You may want to remove the amenities and encourage tenants to use nearby public facilities instead.

Police Reports

What type of property are you buying? Unless you plan on spending several weeks there night and day, it's really hard to get a feel for the property. However, you can get the real truth by pulling police reports. Most police reports can be found online, but you can always call or stop by the police department to obtain that information. By reviewing the police reports, you can truly see what type of property you are buying.

CRITICAL TIP: Police Officer

One of the best security measures you can incorporate is to allow a police officer to live at your property rent free. One stipulation is they must drive their police cruiser home. If you are working to stabilize a property, an established police presence is a great way to accomplish it!

Property Taxes

Always ensure that the property taxes are current. If taxes are not paid to date, there may be fines or penalties assessed. Check with the tax department to confirm when the last assessment was made. Most tax departments reassess property every 5-9 years. If the property is up for reassessment and the taxes go up $3,000 a year, your property is worth $30,000 less, based on a 10% cap rate.

How? Because a $3,000 expense decreases your cash flow by $3,000. If your property taxes are lowered $3,000, then your property is worth $30,000 more based on a 10% cap rate.

Rent Roll

Did you know that a current rent roll ONLY means that a tenant has signed a lease stating they will pay a certain amount? It does NOT mean they are actually paying that amount! Request Bank Statements!

CRITICAL TIP: Rent Roll Nightmare

I purchased a property that — per the rent roll — collected over $28,000 a month. I did all my due diligence and closed on the property. Boy, was I in for a shock! The first month the property only collected $7,000 dollars.

What happened? The rent roll listed the information found on the lease - tenant's name, address, rent, date signed, and maybe a few other things. The rent roll does NOT mean that money is being collected. So, while the rent roll said $28k the property truly only collected $7k a month.

This threw my budget completely out of whack. And this happened because I didn't know what I was doing and I didn't understand the documents I was reviewing.

Range Hoods

Are the range hoods vented? If not, does local code require them to be vented? It would stand to reason that if the range hoods are already installed, then they are compliant. That isn't always the case. Always make sure they are compliant during your due diligence.

Roaches

Roaches can quickly infest a unit and the surrounding units as well. And you won't be able to rent a vacant unit if these pests are present. When walking the occupied units, pay attention to the tenant's kitchens. Are they clean? Are the sinks and counters piled with dirty dishes? It only takes one tenant to help establish a roach colony — and it can cost hundreds if not thousands of dollars to treat it.

Roads: Local and State

Are there any projected road improvement programs? Any planned median additions? Expansion of roads taking away frontage? Is there an interstate planned? The likelihood of this happening may be small, but you never know. And what you don't know will always cost you money.

Roof Structures

What type of roof does the property have? What condition is it in? Is the roof under warranty? How many layers are on the current roof? Roofing is an expensive item.

Have a roofer inspect the roof before your close. If there is more than one layer on the current roof, you will have to remove all of the layers to replace the roof. This is an added expense. You also want a roofer to walk all of the roof structures to check the decking. If the decking is bad, you will definitely need to repair or replace it.

CRITICAL TIP: Documentation

The roof only has a warranty if you have the documentation to prove it or the shingles have a barcode

Security Deposits

Verify the amount on both the leases and rent rolls. Make sure this amount is included in your closing documents.

Sewage

Sewage issues, such as stopped-up toilets can cost hundreds of dollars to unclog. If the toilet overflows, it can cause damage to a lot of other things as well. After purchasing a property, I immediately renovated the two easiest units. They were vacant, the flooring was replaces, and the units were easily renovated.

At six o'clock that evening, I had the final walk through and found standing water in both units. The toilets backed up and water was free flowing throughout both units. I immediately turned the water off and called my plumber. I also called maintenance, and they immediately started extracting the water and removing the flooring. I called the manager who had to call the tenants. I had just lost over $2,000 between the cost of removing and replacing the damaged flooring. And I had also lost $1,200 of rent because I didn't have units to put those tenants in. That was $3,200 down the "toilet."

The plumber ran the snake all the way down the line and just 10 feet short of hitting the city connection, his snake stopped. The next day, they dug up the spot and found a single tree root that had penetrated the sewage line. Water could flow until things like toilet paper got caught on the root. When this happened, the water would back up.

Obviously you can't snake every line during due diligence because it would cost thousands of dollars. What else can you do? How can you determine if a unit or building has a toilet(s) that are backing up?

First talk with the owner, tenants, and maintenance personnel. They might be honest or they might not. The second and best option is to pull the city complaints over the last 24 months and see if any tenants have complained about toilets backing up or have had standing water in their bathtubs. This simple step could save you a few hundred dollars or tens of thousands of dollars.

If a main sewage line is crushed, collapsed or has tree roots growing through it, your budget will be blown — especially if the sewage line is under a concrete foundation.

Sidewalks

If the property has sidewalks, what condition are they in and who is responsible for maintaining them? Both the housing authority and insurance company will inspect them. If the owner is responsible for sidewalk upkeep, then make sure they are in good condition. If they are not in good shape, then negotiate with the seller regarding the cost of fixing them.

Signage

Is there a sign ordinance? What size signs are allowed or not allowed? Don't spend thousands of dollars on signs only to learn that you have to take them down.

Is a permit needed to put your signs up? If you don't pull a permit and put them up, then you will have to still pull the permits and possible pay a fine.

Tenant Applications

How can you verify this? Request copies of all applications for current tenants. This application should include proof of income, a credit report, references, and a signed application. Don't be surprised if these items don't exist. Just be prepared to deal with it at a later date.

CRITICAL TIP: Tenant Screening

Move in the right tenants, and you make money! Move in the wrong tenants, and you lose money! And sleep and friends… and did I mention money? It is critical you do NOT just move in a tenant because they have a security deposit and the first month's rent. I've made enough mistakes regarding tenant selection—and I've also paid the price. During your due diligence, make sure the management company or manager has pre-screened any current tenants.

If prospective tenants have not been pre-screened, then you have to assume that these tenants have no vested interest in protecting their security deposit or credit.

Termites

If you see termites or suspect termite damage, call a termite company. Have a technician inspect the property and suggest what work needs to be done to exterminate and repair the damage. Termites are a pesky and expensive problem. It's worth having someone inspect your property for any termite damage. Find a company that will do a free inspection and provide you with a quote.

Toilets

Two things you need to do here. One, visual inspect the toilet and determine if it needs to be replaced. Second, sit on the toilet! Close the lid first! Is the toilet stable? It could just be the toilet needs to be tightened OR the floor could be rotten.

Vacant Units

The owner should have a list of repairs needed for any vacant units. During your walk-through, compare what the current owner says needs to be fixed to what you see needs to be fixed. This gives you a good indication of how the owner views the property and there record keeping.

Vendor Contracts

Normally when you buy a property, you are bound by all existing contracts. This can be very dangerous and costly if you don't verify all contracts and make sure the seller signs off that no other contracts exist. Your agreement should state that if other contracts exist, then the seller is responsible for any termination fees. Some contracts can get expensive, such as cable contracts. The property may be providing free cable in the rent structure and paying the monthly bill. Landscaping contracts providing year-round services can also be expensive.

Water Damage

When walking the units, look for water stains on the ceilings. Determine what caused the stains. Is there a current or previous leak? Has the water caused mold or mildew to grow?

Work Orders

Obtaining 12 months of past work orders is a great way to see what's going on at the property. If the current owner says they haven't kept them, then either they are disorganized or they don't want you to see the issues. So, to find out what's going on at the property here is what you do.

Zoning Letter

A zoning letter is a legally recognized document which informs commercial property owners, lenders and prospective buyers of zoning laws related to the particular property. You will hear "this property is grandfathered in" meaning the property doesn't meet current zoning laws. Getting a letter from the zoning department confirms IN WRITING that the property is legal to operate as a property. If you can't secure a letter BUYER BEWARE!

CRITICAL TIP: My Nightmare!

If it looks like a duck, walks like a duck, quacks like a duck, then you can assume it's a duck. Right? I wouldn't! I would want a licensed vet to verify that it's a duck and give me that verification in writing. Why? Because what if you buy that duck and it turns out not to be a duck? Well, that happened to me. I purchased a 24-unit rental property that the surveyor, appraiser and attorney all verified was a 24-unit rental property. I walked the property more than two dozen times — and it had 24 units every time!

But when I went to pull my building permits after closing, I was informed the property had lost its grandfather due to the way the property was split up, and the current building would have to be brought up to current code. What? Huh? But? It didn't matter what I said or who I talked to. The code is the code. It took me 18 months and more than $150k to solve the problem. It was an absolute nightmare! The worst part is I could have avoided it by simply called or going to the zoning board and requested a written verification

Before you submit an offer on a property, check with the zoning department and verify compliance and get it in writing. If there is an issue down the road, you have documentation from the zoning department!

PERSONAL STORY:
What You Can't See...

Most of the mistakes I've made in my life were my mistakes of my own doing. I honestly didn't mean to step into the middle of something, but in hindsight I also didn't do everything I could have to avoid stepping in the middle of it. So while I didn't mean to create a problem, I also didn't avoid it to the best of my ability.

This was certainly true my sophomore year in college. I had grown up driving a truck in a muddy field from the time I could steer and reach the pedals. My granddad would take us to the farm and turn me lose! Most of the time, he would get out of the truck and sit on a stump and watch. It was a blast.

Then in the early 90s, I owned a brand-new Chevrolet Z71. It was January in Laurinburg, North Carolina, and it has just rained. The picture was perfect. A few of my buddies jumped in my truck and off we went. Mud flying everywhere! Spinning around and around, and just having an awesome time!

The next morning, I awoke to a loud bang on my door. When I opened the door, two of Laurinburg's finest were standing there with the most serious look I think I've ever seen.

"Mr. Tabor, do you drive a burgundy Chevrolet Z71? And were you mudding yesterday?"

"Yes, sir. That was me."

"Mr. Tabor, you need to come with us."

About 30 minutes later, I found out that I had done around $1,500 dollars of damage to a farmer's winter wheat field. I had thought that it was just an empty field because there wasn't anything visible but dirt. But underneath the ground, the seeds had started to sprout and would be ready to harvest mid-spring.

I felt horrible. I had grown up on a farm, and I probably should have known better. I apologized and made restitution to the farmer. However, had I been where I was supposed to be, this wouldn't have happened. I really didn't have an excuse.

The same rings true if you purchase a property and don't do your due diligence. You need to dig deep to find what's under the surface.

Documents to Request from the Seller (if applicable)

- Bank Statements (12-24 months)
- Expenses
- P&L
- Zoning Letter
- Statement of Policies Governing HUD Communities
- Site Layout
- Floor Plan of Units (with square footage)
- Tenant-Screening Process
- Tenant Application Packet
- Model Lease
- Facility Condition Reports
- HVAC Maintenance Reports
- Roof Warranty Paperwork
- Last 2 Years of Financials
- Current Rent Roll

- Tenant Payment Ledger
- Last 12 Months of Evictions
- Vacant Units (with repairs needed)
- City Complaints
- Last 12 Months of Work Orders
- Copy of All Leases
- Copy of All Current Tenant Applications
- Security Deposits
- Executed Vendor Contracts

This is a comprehensive list of documents, issues and topics but each deal is unique. Please make sure you request any and all documents you may need. Walk every unit, examine every contract, turn over every stone – do everything you can to verify, get everything in writing and always consult an attorney.

About Nathan Tabor

Nathan Tabor has built a life helping others and improving lives. Throughout his own life and experiences, Nathan has acquired an incredible ability to solve problems, develop game plans, and create real and lasting results in both his personal and professional life.

He has successfully founded and operated more than two dozen businesses since 1999, grossing over $150 million in sales. His experience spans the areas of commercial real estate acquisition and redevelopment, automobile sales, direct product sales, web-based marketing, and strategic partnership facilitation.

Real Estate Experience

- 26 Properties Flipped in 9 years
- Grossed over $52 million in sales
- Raised over $1 million from investors
- Consulted on deals worth over $200 million
- Author, The Guide to Due Diligence

- Author, The Guide to Defining Your Niche
- Author, How to Find, Finance, Fix & Flip Apartments
- Author, Achieving Balance

He's had amazing successes and epic failures, and learned more from his failures than his successes. After years of struggling to keep all of the balls in the air, he learned that there are laws and processes that, when implemented, will deliver the desired results.

Over the years, his companies have been honored with many awards and rankings. In 2012, 2013 and 2104 his parent company was ranked by Inc. magazine's Inc. 5000 as one of the fastest growing small businesses in the United States. In 2014, 2015, and 2016, his real estate management company was listed as one of the largest in the Piedmont Triad.

Nathan earned his Bachelor's degree in Psychology from St. Andrew's Presbyterian College and his Master's degree in Public Policy from Regent University. He has been married to Jordan since December 2003 and their daughter Abigail was born in January 2005.

Services Offered

No matter your real estate goals—buying, selling, renovating, securing funds or flipping—as an experienced and knowledgeable consultant, I will help bring opportunities into focus and develop a plan of action. You'll gain the experience, know-how, and strategic planning to help you avoid the many pitfalls of the real estate business. And you'll take away actionable items that you can implement in your business today!

Services offered:

- ✓ Brainstorming session: This is a one-hour session with Nathan designed to answer and/or discuss any topics. Ranging from where you should start or how to deal with a specific issue.

- ✓ Coaching: Nathan will walk you through a series of exercises from setting your goals, developing your business plan to expanding your business.

- ✓ Consulting: From finding a deal, engaging a real estate broker, structuring a deal, approaching an investor, submitting a loan request to any part of a real estate deal Nathan can assist you.

- ✓ Work-Life Balance Program: As you know, it's critical for people to have a healthy work-life balance. That means managing your professional life alongside your personal life in a healthy way. Why? Because stress and anxiety affect a person's ability to function at their best.

- ✓ Analyzing Deals: This involves all aspects of the deal ranging from reviewing the purchase contract, rent rolls, comps, expenses and leases to analyzing the P&L's, comps and cap rate. Nathan will then provide you with a report identifying any areas of concern. Finding an error or correcting an error can swing your deal by tens of thousands if not hundreds of thousands of dollars.

- ✓ Flipping Deals: Nathan will help you package your deal to take to market. First impressions matter the most. The strength of your packet sets the tone for negotiating the sale.

- ✓ Finance/Refinance: There are numerous options available: Construction Loans, Acquisition Loans, Cash

Out Refinance, Renovation Loans and many other options.

- ✓ Due Diligence: Don't have the time to walk every unit or worried you might miss something? Nathan can help you will a particular part of due diligence or he can do all of the due diligence for you.

Interested in working with Nathan? Send an email to Nathan@NathanTabor.com

Disclaimer

All material contained in this book is provided for educational and informational purposes only. No responsibility can be taken for any results or outcomes resulting from the use of this material. While every attempt has been made to provide information that is both accurate and effective, the author and publisher do not assume any responsibility for the accuracy or use and/or misuse of the information herein. The author and publisher do not guarantee that anyone following these techniques, suggestions, tips, ideas, or strategies will become successful. The author and publisher shall have neither liability nor responsibility to anyone with respect to any loss or damage caused or alleged to be caused directly or indirectly by the information contained in this book.

www.ingramcontent.com/pod-product-compliance
Lightning Source LLC
Chambersburg PA
CBHW030734180526
45157CB00008BA/3168